Mind Sparks

Kandace Scott

BookLeaf
Publishing

India | USA | UK

Presentation by *BookLeaf Publishing*

Web: www.bookleafpub.com

E-mail: info@bookleafpub.com

ISBN: 9789358317206

First edition 2024

Little things

It's the little things
That provide so much joy
 beauty that surrounds
The senses that sing

The beauty of the stars
Blowing of a gentle breeze
Fields of all colors
A fragrant flower
Weeping willows in the wind
The canvas of sunrise and sunset
The rolling mountains
The rivers, lakes & streams
The rainbow of fresh fall leaves
Bonfires burning bright
beautiful art for all to enjoy

A sweet melody
A beat that transcends
Lyrics that take you to another time
A song that speaks to the heart

The brush stroke
Swirling colors of beauty
Capturing tranquility

Intriguing the mind
Image captured in time

A sweet gesture
That first sip of coffee
The inhale of herbal tea
The memories of childhood

A soft whisper
Wrapped in someone's arms
The peace of contentment
A listening ear
Connected souls
Conversations with a friend
Losing the world around you

Sometimes

Sometimes it's hard to carry
Those emotions left behind
The residue of crisis
All the thoughts of someone else's mind

Sometimes it's hard to face
The absolute misery
The no answer to be had
The things aren't always what you see

Sometimes it's hard to separate
The you tries to drown me
Have to purge what isn't mine
Some days like that it just be

Some days there's just lots of pain to be found
And the evil in the world rears it's head
But at the end of all these sometimes
It's still where I'm being led

The truth is sometimes it's beautiful and others
it's not
Some situations are pretty bad
But there's always a light to be seen
A lesson to be had

At the end of the day I'm thankful to help
To be a listening ear
To plant the seeds of different thought
And for all the successes I hear

I'm thankful for the families
The lives I'm allowed to share
The being able to see the progress
To be the person they know will care

Healing

From church to another galaxy
Floating through space
Lost in the moment
In a whole other universe
Exploration

Overcome in peace
Beautiful melodies
Soothing tones
Calming presence
Release

Dancing to the beat
Flowing freely
Shaking off the absorption
Clearing all thought
Immersion

Adventures

The mountains are calling
And my heart is at peace
Enjoying the beauty all around
The stress is melting away
As I take in the beautiful scene
And breathe a breath of nature
The music is playing and with you I can sing
My heart is open and free
Utter tranquility

Through the twists I wander
Climbing over the roots
Blazing a new trail
Exploring all the world has to offer
Testing the limits even if with caution
Finding, learning, growing
Expanding the possibilities
Excavation of the spirit
Connecting and grounding
Utmost adventure

Masterpiece

The magic that is us swirls around
The feelings, the sights, the sound
We are like a mosiac of the things we have done
A beautiful pattern of the mundane and the fun
Pieces of light and love
The experiences we are made up of
The special moments each add
Not only the good but also the bad
Each event creating more art
Like a kaleidoscope of our heart
The beauty of nature, the moon and the stars
Add to the background of the beauty that is ours
The music the soundtrack that memories hold
The sharing of the mind that never gets old
We are a masterpiece each in our own way
Adding brush strokes each and every day

Motherhood

Time flies by and the days go fast
Before you know it so much has passed
Things change and children grow
And along you go with the flow
The memories of days past remain
Some of joy and some of pain
Living, loving, sharing the days
Won't be long until the new phase
Are you ready, am I
Will we succeed at the new things we try
This is a time of transition, a season in time
To not feel the joy would be a crime
I'm so proud of you two and who you have
became
So very different but kindness the same
I love your hearts for others and to see you be
you
I hope you learn to love yourself just as much
too
The beauty you create in this world through
what you give
I can't wait to see this amazing life you live
Follow your heart and always feel love
My wish for you is everything you dream of

Beauty

I love to be lost in the moment
And the feeling it brings
That moment of total freedom
The ones where my heart sings

I love the beauty of nature
The night sky
The mountains and streams
Sunsets that make you sigh

I love good music
The melodies and the beat
The places the song can take me
The way into it I can retreat

I love the stories
The rawness of the share
To know what makes people who they are
The chance to show care

All the magic in the moments
The feelings you can't explain
The losing of inhibitions
The dancing in the rain

I love the flowers
The beautiful colors and smell
The individuality of each one
Even the story they can tell

I love art
The way it swirls and flows
The catching of a moment
To observe what image someone chose

So many miss the beauty
Miss the forest for the trees
Not aware of the awe
Just going through life to appease

May I never overlook the little things
The beauty all around me
May you never miss it either
My wish for you is to also see

Reconstruction

The words ring so true
I feel them to the core
Description of exactly how I feel
How I can't feel anymore

I allowed myself to get in that position
And broke my own heart
Now it's time to put it back together
To pick up each part

To accept that I can love and be loved
And don't have to continue to fear
To know it's most important to love me
The outside influences to clear

Just because you want it
Doesn't make it easy to do
Digging up these things will be hard
But it is necessary too

Being

I want to be among the wildflowers
I want to be lost in the moments in time
I want one of those times of talking for hours
I want to pause the climb

I long for the time to slow down
Time to enjoy nature too
The people that take away a frown
The days without checklists to do

I want to sway in the wind
And dance like nobody can see
Reality to transcend
To have the freedom to just be

Thank you

I never seem to have the right words
The way to express what I mean
I guess it's thank you for having me
For the knowledge that I can feel safe
For the ability to just lean because I have
complete faith in you
For the friendship that helps to heal
With each wall I drop I find more debri left
holding on
Then take time to clean that out as well
I never realized how much I held so tight that
needed to be purged
Thank you for the smiles
As I fight through the hard
As I examine what I know and what I still need
to
As I unbury myself from the junk
For the support and encouragement like no other
Thank you for showing my girls that sometimes
it's ok to trust and for showing me that too
And for understanding that sometimes I just
don't have the words
But I always want to try to

Music

Every song a memory
A moment caught in time
Each melody a feeling
Each lyric a thought

The special people
Days gone past
Each rhythm flowing through
Bringing with it peace

Every remember when
Flowing through the chords
Drifting in time
Soothing the rough edges

Each touch to my soul
A story there is held
A chapter in the life
Flowing through the mind

Magic

There is magic in the process
The baring of souls
The sharing of the hard stuff
The way life rolls

There is magic in the beauty
Of the vulnerability
The willingness to share
The pointing out of ability

There is magic in the healing
The making once again whole
The finding the peace
The letting go of control

There is magic in the broken pieces
The ones we handle with care
The changes in perspective
And the peace we find there

There is magic in it all you see
The love and the joy and the pain
There is magic within all of us
If in the magical moments we remain

Kaitlyn

Beautiful soul
Don't hide away
Embrace who you are
Be who you dream

Love with all your heart
Feel with all your soul
Don't be swayed
Embrace the greatness

I know it hurts
Pain so real
Judging words
Looks of disgust
Misunderstanding

Beautiful soul
Don't let them win
Be who you are
Embrace your dreams

Lily

Beautiful soul, kind heart
Lover of animals and kids
So insightful and so smart
Sweet spirt, strong resolve.
My beautiful eldest words can't express the
pride I feel for you,
I'm so blessed to be your mom,
You go above and beyond in all you do.
Big hearted caregiver,
Worrier of all
Always know your worth.
Believe in yourself
Never settle for less
These things I wish for you my love!
You are amazing, brilliant, and kind
Let your light shine bright in this world
Be cautious but darling be fearless
Know that you have a purpose only you can
fulfill
This world is tough and will try to knock you
down
But you my dear are tougher
Make sure to straighten your crown.
My rock & roll princess
March to the beat of your own drum

Take the time to enjoy yourself
And never forget where you come from.
You my dear are special
There is no one quite like you
Go into this big world
And show them all just what you can do.

Finding my soul

Finding my soul in the fresh mountain air
In the rolling of the hills
In the beauty of the night
The weeping of the willow

In the melody of the song
In the beat getting lost
In the moment singing along
The memories wrapped in each one

In the adventures
In the exploring
In the ordinary & extraordinary
Being present, making memories

In the beauty of it all
In the art of the created
In nature, music, art, and life
The loving, the living, the joy

Taking back me

Dissipation, frustration, fading to the core
Once I was lost but now no more
Drowning in the expectation
Always trying to please
Caring so much about others
Bringing me to my knees
Part of the broken system
Longing to make a change
Burdened with so much evil
More jaded with each case
Fighting, constantly running the race
Doing it all for me and for you
Always being the one who knew what to do
This life it took a part of me
changed the person I used to be
And now I fight in a different way
Time to take back me today

My all

I wouldn't change a thing
Not one single tear
Every heartbreak and devestation brought me
here

I layed it all down
I got in the ring
At the end of the day that's everything

Never may I know if a seed grew
Never may I see the end
But I don't need to that is the beauty my friend

I gave all I had
I fought the good fight
Always advocated for what is right

Now it's time to move on
Different battles new call
At the end of the day I gave it my all

Light after the dark

Light after the dark
Calm after the storm
You are the peace
That little bit of norm

Not where you have been
Not what you have done
Beautiful as the stars
Bright as the sun

The whisper in the wind
The melody of the song
You are the wildflower
The one for which I long

The shade of the willow
The babbling of the brook
The heat of a summer day
The all it takes is a look

The beat of a heart
The tranquility of the fields
The rush of a waterfall
The makes me fall apart

Want

I want to know your soul
I want to talk for hours
I want to feel your pain
I want to see your reality

It's the little things
The small glance, the kind word
That makes my heart soar
The lost in the moment
Nobody else but you kinda nights

I want to watch the stars
I want to hear your song
Tell me your fears,your truth
On this journey take me along

Give me the unmasked truth
Lay it all on the line
Let me truly in
Make the memories that really shine

Impact

How has it impacted my life
In so many ways you see
It has given me back my sense of adventure
My ability to explore pain free
It's given me community
A place that feels like home to me
It's given me more confidence
And the ability to just be
Better health and less weight
A whole new group of friends
The ability to love in a way I thought I lost
And memories without ends
Insight about myself
Encouragement from all around
A love for being active
And amazing people abound
The freedom to take more risk
A life with more joy
Some amazing conversations
And new things to enjoy
So much more than I can even express
Growth and healing too
One small decision made all the difference
And for that I thank you

Unbreakable

I never realized
I guess I was blind
Never paid attention
Couldn't see past the tears I have cried
Never saw how special I was
Or what I could really do
After all I was told nobody would love me
Which was oh so very untrue
But here I am thriving
Growing more and more each day
Here I am happy
So thankful I got away
Things worked out well for me
Not one regret
Because I am a force to be reckoned with
And I'm not close to being done yet